Concerning Them Which Are Asleep

Victory and Hope for the Dead in Christ

by
Dr. Frederick K.C. Price

Unless otherwise indicated, all Scripture quotations are taken from the *King James Version* of the Bible.

Concerning Them Which Are Asleep:
Victory and Hope for the Dead in Christ
ISBN 0-89274-603-3
Copyright © 1989 by Dr. Frederick K.C. Price
Crenshaw Christian Center
P.O. Box 90000
Los Angeles, California 90009

Printed in the United States of America.
All rights reserved under International Copyright Law. Contents and/or cover may not be reproduced in whole or in part in any form without the express written consent of the Publisher.

Concerning Them Which Are Asleep

Victory and Hope for the Dead in Christ

For many people, death is a morbid subject which they don't even want to think about, and certainly not talk about. However, the Bible-informed Christian knows that death, although an enemy, has no sting, nor the grave any victory. (1 Cor. 15:26,55.) In fact, the Bible refers to those Christians who have died as being asleep.

> But I would not have you to be ignorant, brethren, concerning them which are asleep, that ye sorrow not, even as others which have no hope.
>
> 1 Thessalonians 4:13

This statement, to me, is so very beautiful. If God does not want us, His children, to be ignorant, then the opposite of that would be that He wants us to be informed. Therefore, if we are ignorant, it's our fault — not God's. He wants us to have knowledge about the things that affect us spiritually; that's why He gave us the Bible.

Now there are those who, even though they have the Bible, are still ignorant, and that is a real tragedy. It is one thing not to have The Book and be ignorant, but to have it in your home and then be ignorant is a travesty of justice. It is, however, easy to understand why that would be the case, since most people by nature are followers rather than leaders.

If believers are not taught, if they are not spiritually informed, and if the importance of knowing and studying God's Word is not stressed to them, then they will go along with the flow of whatever is being taught at the time. That's why there are multitudes of Christians who are ignorant of who they are in Christ, ignorant of what Christ has done for them, ignorant of what He is doing for them now, ignorant of what He wants for them, and ignorant of what He has actually provided for them through the covenant He has established with the Father God on our behalf.

From a careful study of God's Word, it is very clear that He does not want us to be ignorant about our spiritual life. Based on that fact, it is a presupposition that whatever it takes to nullify that ignorance is available to us. Otherwise, it would be pointless for God to want us to be spiritually informed and then not make available to us the tools necessary to do away with the ignorance that is keeping us spiritually blind.

I personally believe that I don't have to be ignorant of the things of God. You have to personalize this also. You have to go beyond your church, your minister, your spouse, your parents, your children, your girlfriend, boyfriend, fiance, dog, cat, or whatever. You have to go beyond everybody and decide for yourself that spiritual knowledge is for you; even if it's not for anyone else on this planet, it's for you. You have to make it personal, because God deals with each one of us on an individual basis. He also deals with us collectively, but in the end the bottom line is: "It's me and the Lord."

> **For if we believe that Jesus died and rose again, even so them also which sleep in Jesus will God bring with him.**
> **1 Thessalonians 4:14**

The word "sleep" as used in verses 13 and 14 of this passage is a synonym for the word "death." In other words, God views His children as being asleep when they die.

We humans think of people as being only what we see with our natural, physical eyes. When what we see with our natural eyes ceases to be animated or alive, then that person or thing is what we call dead. When a person dies, we think that individual has ceased to exist. However, God considers only the physical part of that person as being asleep.

There are several scriptures that give credence to this. In John 11:11 Jesus, talking about Lazarus, who had died, said, "I'm going to wake Lazarus out of his sleep." Again, in speaking of Jairus' 12-year-old daughter, He said that she was not dead, but was asleep. (Matt. 9:24.) Then we read in 1 Corinthians 15:51,52:

> ...We shall not all sleep, but we shall all be changed,
>
> In a moment, in the twinkling of an eye, at the last trump: for the trumpet shall sound, and the dead shall be raised incorruptible, and we shall be changed.

There are two important things relative to sleep which have no fear associated with them at all. Yet death, as it is portrayed in the world — primarily the western world — is a very traumatic event. To most people, death is a "tear-jerker." It is a heart-rending, mind-boggling, terrifying experience. It should not be this way for us Christians — not if we have been properly taught what the Word of God says about it.

This is not to say that there will not be natural feelings of loss in the sense that the person known and loved will no longer be there for us to have personal, physical contact or fellowship with. There is a natural sense of loss because a separation has occurred; however, this separation should be like that which we experience when someone we love — perhaps a close relative or a very dear friend — has to leave after a wonderful, warm visit. Often that is a very emotionally upsetting moment for us, knowing that we won't see one another for a long time.

However, this is not a despairing kind of separation or discomfort. There is no sense of hopelessness, because it is not as if we will never see each other again. This is how the Christian should view the death of another believer. Yet, this is not the way most believers feel about death, and it is mainly because of not having been taught the Word concerning Christian death.

In fact, many believers have come to expect unbearable, emotional pain, just like that experienced by anybody else. God, however, says that when Christians die, they are asleep. When somebody is asleep, two great things are implied: 1) *he is going to wake up*, and 2) *he should wake up rested*.

Sleep is designed to allow the body a chance to recuperate and to re-energize. We ought to think of death this way.

Over the years, since finding out how to walk by faith, I have had to deal with my own thinking about death. Since I discovered what death really is all about, when I have to preach a funeral, or even attend one, I experience almost a sense of guilt because I don't feel like weeping all over the place or going all to pieces. It's not that I am not thinking about the person I will never see again on this side of what we call life, but because I know that death is not the end. I feel almost guilty when I see some people at funerals who are all torn up, and I'm not. If you don't know what God's Word has to say about the subject, death can be an awesome, terrible situation to face.

I remember when my little boy was killed many years ago by an automobile, I went through all kinds of devastating emotions. I cried so, until I thought my heart was going to break. In fact, for quite a long time after his death, I could not even talk about my son, because it hurt too much to do so. Now, because I know what the Bible says, I can talk about this painful time in my life and Betty's.

At the time of my son's death, the churches I had attended had not told me what the Bible says about Christian death. Consequently, it was unbearable for me to even think about my son being dead. I don't get all torn up inside anymore when I think about the believers who have passed on, because I know they're not dead! They are asleep, and the alarm clock is set. One of these days, it's going to ring, and when it does, the sleepers are going to arise! Praise God!

The Bible says that God is the God of the living because there is no death in Him, in terms of a person ceasing to exist. There is no such thing as people ceasing to exist. They are simply "put on hold" for a while.

For example, when I put on my clothes, they become alive with my movements — my suit, my shoes, my socks, my tie — all move with my movements. In other words, they are alive with my movements. But when I take off my clothes and place them on a hanger in my closet, they are no longer alive with movement; they just hang there — no life in them at all. What has happened is that the life that was causing the movement in the suit, the shoes, the socks, the tie, was not in the clothes, but in the one wearing them.

Well, the one wearing our physical clothes (our bodies) is the spirit man on the inside. He wears the physical body as a suit of clothes in this three-dimensional world. When you and I enter into that state of what we call death, all he (the spirit man) does is hang up the clothes (the physical body) in the closet (the grave or whatever place has become the temporary resting place).

That suit that is hanging on the rack in the closet is sleeping, it is resting; it has not ceased to exist. My suit will come alive again. One day, it is going to become alive once more. One day, I'm going into the closet and take this suit out and wear it. It will be alive again — it will be moving again. People will look down the street and say: "Look at that! There goes Fred Price's gray suit. Look at it! Wow! Look at that suit move!" They will say that because I will be in it!

The Christian's suit (his body) will come alive again, because the spirit will once again wear it.

Let's look at 1 Thessalonians 4:13 again. I want to discuss something else that is significant concerning the "others" mentioned in this verse: "But I would not have you to be ignorant, brethren, concerning them which are asleep, that ye sorrow not, *even as others, which have no hope.*"

The "others" spoken of here are non-Christians; they have no hope. For them — the non-believers — death is an end. For the non-Christian, yes, death is traumatic; it is an agony. I have known of cases where some loved one has died, and the grieving person did not have hope because he or she did not know what we know from the Word of God. I have seen people literally die themselves in a very short period of time after the loss of a loved one. They could not deal with that person's death. It was too traumatic for them. That happened because they had no hope.

Man: Spirit, Soul and Body

Man is a tripartite being. The real you is a spirit, you have a soul (which consists of your mind, will and emotions), and you live inside a physical body. In what we call "death," there is no loss of identity and awareness, spiritually speaking. I am talking about the man on the inside — the spirit man. Let's look at some scriptures that validate this fact:

> **For we know that if our earthly house of this tabernacle were dissolved, we have a building of God, an house not made with hands, eternal in the heavens.**
> **2 Corinthians 5:1**

Now notice that the Apostle Paul says, "For we know that if *'our* earthly *house'*..." — so it is obvious from this statement that there are two separate concepts under discussion here: "our" and "house." "Our" refers to the owner or possessor. The "house" is the object of possession. That means that the persons (us) to which the word "our" refers must be separate and distinct from the "house" in which those persons live.

"For we know that if our *earthly* house..." Now right away this implies that there must be another kind of house. If this were the only house, then Paul would not have said "earthly" — we only say "earthly" to distinguish from "heavenly." If there were only one kind of house, Paul would not have needed to specify that he was speaking of an "earthly" house.

For in this (that is, in this "earthly house") **we groan** ("we" meaning the persons referred to by the word "our" in verse 1 — the real us), **earnestly desiring to be clothed upon with our house which is from heaven.**

2 Corinthians 5:2

First, Paul talks about our earthly house, then he talks about another house, which he says is from heaven.

(If you will re-read these two verses, mentally substituting "our spirit man's" for "our," "physical body" for "earthly house of this tabernacle," and "our heavenly spirit" for "our house which is from heaven," it will help you get a picture of the image Paul is conveying here about the relationship between the physical body and the immortal spirit.)

If so be that being clothed we shall not be found naked.

For we that are in this tabernacle do groan, being burdened: not for that we

would be unclothed (in other words, we do not want to be unclothed), **but clothed upon, that mortality might be swallowed up of life.**

2 Corinthians 5:3,4

What Paul is telling us here is that we are groaning for the greater end. Now that does not mean that we do not want to live in the earthly house, because we do — it is really the only house we know anything about. The heavenly house we take by faith. But experientially we are living in this earthly house. We have been doing so for a number of years, so we are very used to this house. The heavenly house we are not used to. However, the inner man (the spirit man) groans for that heavenly house because the inner man knows that it is the ultimate house — and a better one.

"...that *mortality* might be swallowed up of life." The word "mortality" refers to death or dying.

Now he that hath wrought us for the selfsame thing is God, who also hath given unto us the earnest of the Spirit.

2 Corinthians 5:5

Now "the earnest of the Spirit" means "the down payment." When we were born again, we received the down payment on our salvation. The Holy Spirit came into us to take up residence as Christ's representative. I am not talking about being filled with the Spirit, I am talking about being born of the Spirit. The Holy Spirit is the One Who comes into us as Christ's representative to cause the New Birth to take place. That is the down payment of our total salvation package. The other installment will include a brand-new body and a brand-new soul.

Therefore we are always confident, knowing that, whilst we are at home in the body (our earthly house, our home in this realm), **we are absent from the Lord** (because the Lord is in heaven):

(For we walk by faith, not by sight.)
2 Corinthians 5:6,7

Paul is saying that we have to take all of this by faith, because we cannot see our heavenly house, but by faith we receive it.

> We are confident, I say, and willing rather to be absent from the body, and to be present with the Lord.
>
> **2 Corinthians 5:8**

Now when you are absent from and present with, that means you are *present with* and *absent from*. You need to read that very carefully. There is no such thing as not being somewhere all the time. You can't be nowhere; you have to be somewhere. When you die, you (in the form of your spirit man) are either in heaven (if you have accepted Jesus as Lord and Savior), or you are in hell (if you have not received Jesus). After you leave this earth, you have to be in either one place or the other. This verse does not leave room for saying that you are "on your way." The Bible says that to be absent from is to be present with. It *does not say* to be present with is to be on the way.

This epistle was written to the children of God. A child of God is one who has personally acknowledged and accepted Jesus Christ as his Savior and Lord. It is not somebody who believes in the legend of Jesus, but someone who has made Jesus Christ the Lord of his life. That person is what the Bible calls "born again," "a new creature in Christ," "saved," "a Christian." If one of these titles does not apply to you, then for you to be absent from the body *is not* to be present with the Lord Jesus. If you are not a child of God, then to be absent from the body is to be present with the devil, because he is your lord. If Jesus is your Lord, then for you to be absent from the body is to be present with Him. If you are not a Christian, then to be absent from the body is to be with your lord, Satan. If Jesus is not your Lord, then the devil is, whether you know it or not.

You may be an adopted child, in the natural world, and you may not know who your biological mother is — the one whose womb you came out of. You may have been taken from her, or she may have given you away. You may never know in this life who your natural mother is; but that does not make any difference, she is still your mother. She is not your mother because you know her, she is your mother because she gave birth to you. Likewise, as long as you are alive on this earth, you may not know that Satan is your lord, but you will surely know it when you die, because to be absent from the body is to be present with "the lord." The question is: which lord is your lord?

"We are confident, I say, and willing rather to be absent from the body and be present with the Lord." This verse of scripture is talking about death, in the sense that when we die, our spirits with our souls leave our bodies and go to be with the Lord or to be with Satan.

There is a teaching called the doctrine of purgatory. I am not attempting to defame any person or group. I am only attempting to clarify this verse with reference to being absent from and present with. Now, with regard to this doctrine of purgatory, my understanding of it is that purgatory is an intermediate place between earth and heaven. If a person is not quite good enough (whatever "good enough" is) to go directly from earth to heaven, he goes to this intermediate state. His relatives and friends and the church must then pray him out of purgatory and into heaven.

This is a doctrine invented by men. I don't say that to put down anybody, but we have a choice either to believe man or to believe what the Word of God says. No one can be prayed out of purgatory because, according to the Bible, there is no such place. If one is teaching something, then there should be a basis for what is being taught, a basis which is verifiable by some higher authority — which in this case would be the Word of God. This doctrine is not in any Bible, not even in the Bible used by the denomination that supports this teaching. There is no such place as purgatory, or limbo. The Bible says, "To be absent from the body is to be present with the Lord."

There is another teaching called the doctrine of "soul sleep" which is subscribed to by another denomination. According to this theory, when a person dies, his body is dead, and his soul goes to sleep.

There is no such teaching in the Bible. If there were a single scripture to indicate that the soul goes to sleep, then it would verify this doctrine. But there is none. Rather, there is scripture to the contrary that discredits this theory.

The book of Revelation was written by the Apostle John, who also authored the Gospel of John and the three epistles accredited to him. He was the last of the twelve apostles who actually walked with Jesus on the earth during His ministry. In Revelation he describes a vision he had while on the island of Patmos, where he had been exiled because of his witness and testimony of Jesus.

While on this island, John wrote the Apocalypse (which means "revelation"), describing the vision he had received pertaining to the ministry and person of Jesus Christ. In presenting this vision, John states:

> **I was in the Spirit on the Lord's day....**
> **Revelation 1:10**

While he was in this state, John's spirit and soul left his body under God's direction, and he was taken up into heaven where he saw a throne and the One Who sat upon it, as well as other things relative to the spirit realm. He describes a book with several seals, and he tells about what happened when each of these seals was broken. Then he saw the four riders, called the "four horsemen of the Apocalypse." Finally, he saw Jesus take the book:

> And when he had opened the fifth seal, I saw under the altar *the souls of them* that were slain for the word of God, and for the testimony which they held.
>
> Revelation 6:9

Notice, "souls *of* them." Remember, "our earthly house." John did not say, "I saw them"; he said, "I saw the souls *of* them." A spirit cannot die. It is impossible to slay a soul. The only part of the human being which can be killed is his physical body. John did not say that he saw *them* who had been slain, but rather he saw the souls *of* them who had been slain.

> And they cried with a loud voice, saying, How long, O Lord, holy and true, dost thou not judge and avenge our blood on them that dwell on the earth?
>
> And white robes were given unto every one of them; and it was said unto them, that they should rest yet for a little season,

until their fellowservants also and their brethren, that should be killed as they were, should be fulfilled.

Revelation 6:10,11

John saw the souls of the martyrs of God, and they cried. That means that they had to be alive. They had to have life in order to be able to cry out. They had loud voices. They cried and asked, "How long, O Lord?" The Bible says that white robes were given to them. You cannot put a robe on an object that has no shape or form. Therefore, spirits and souls have shape and form just as God does. God is a spirit. (John 4:24.)

It was God, Who is a spirit, Who told Moses on Mount Sinai that no man could see His face and live. That means He must have a face to be seen.

We think of spirits as not having material substance. They do have substance; however, it is a different kind of substance from anything we know about. For example, it is like the wave length on an FM broadcast or transmission which is different from an AM broadcast or transmission. It is possible to have two programs — one on FM and the other on AM — being broadcast at the same time, a simulcast, yet it would not be possible to pick up one broadcast on the other frequency. You would either have to pick up the FM broadcast on an FM receiver, or the AM broadcast on an AM receiver.

Spirits have substance, but it is different from the substance of our physical bodies. But it is a substance nonetheless. There is shape and form, and there is structure.

If John saw the souls, then there would have to have been something for him to see, otherwise how could he have known that these souls were under the altar? He pinpointed a specific location. He did not say in front of the altar, or on top of the altar, He said *under* the altar.

He also said that white robes were given to them. He did not just say "robes" — he said that they were *white* robes, so there must be color in the spirit world.

The soul goes right on living — not sleeping. These souls belonged to bodies that had been slain. These souls went right on living.

They had consciousness. They had memory. They had voices, and they had form.

The Bible says that when a Christian dies, he goes to sleep. When he goes to sleep, his body is the only part of him that does so. The spirit, with its soul, leaps out of the body through the mouth, and goes right on up to the third heaven to be with the Heavenly Father and the Lord Jesus Christ.

"For if we believe that Jesus died and rose again, even so them also which sleep in Jesus will God bring with him." (1 Thess. 4:14.) Now those whom God is going to bring with Jesus are the spirits and souls of all the believers who have physically died, those whose physical bodies have gone to sleep. The trumpet will sound, and God will awaken the sleeping bodies. When He awakens them, they will be reunited with their spirits and souls. The souls will be made perfect. The physical bodies will be transformed and made like unto the glorious body that Jesus now has. Then the body, and the soul, and the spirit will be joined together again — never again to be separated. All this will take place in an instant!

There is a scientific principle called the indestructibility of matter. It simply means that matter cannot be destroyed. It can change forms, it can go from a solid to a gas to a liquid, but matter itself actually never goes out of existence. It is still in the universe, and God knows where every atom, every molecule, of it is. All He has to do is clap His hands, snap His fingers, and these atoms and molecules will all come back together.

Some people have been blown up in explosions. They haven't been destroyed — not in the sense of non-existence. God knows where every atom of them is. He made all matter. People may be disembodied, disassembled, but God knows where every part is. When Jesus comes back, and the trumpet sounds, those bodies, through the power of God, will be brought back together from where they are.

The only things that will come up out of the grave are the "earthly houses" (the dead bodies) to be reunited with their "heavenly houses" (their spirits and souls) to live on the earth. The ultimate destiny of man is to live on the earth; that's why you and I need a body. We won't need a body in heaven. Yes, we Christians will live on this earth. The earth will be renovated by fire and made like brand new. This is a beautiful world; it's a beautiful earth. When God has gotten rid of all that man has done to destroy and pollute this planet, it will once again be a wonderful place to live.

Later on in the book of Revelation, John talks about the New Jerusalem coming down from heaven. Where will it come down to? It will come down to earth. In Revelation 21:5, God says, **...Behold, I make all things new....** He did not say that He would make *all new things*! Now in doing that, God calls it a new heaven and a new earth, but when He finishes with this earth, it is going to be restored to the state of the Garden of Eden, as it was before man messed things up.

> **For this we say unto you by the word of the Lord, that we which are alive and remain unto the coming of the Lord shall not prevent them which are asleep.**
> **1 Thessalonians 4:15**

Now in the *King James Version*, this verse says "prevent," but the modern English meaning of this word is "precede." So we shall not precede those who are asleep in Christ. This scripture reveals that man is not going to completely destroy himself from off the planet because the Bible indicates that there will still be people alive, living on earth, when Christ returns.

> For the Lord himself shall descend from heaven with a shout, with the voice of the archangel, and with the trump of God: and the dead in Christ shall rise first:
>
> Then we which are alive and remain shall be caught up together with them (that is, with the dead in Christ who have already risen) in the clouds, to meet the Lord in the air: and so shall we ever be with the Lord.
> 1 Thessalonians 4:16,17

Notice that this verse tells us that we are going to meet the Lord in the clouds, but it does not say that we are going to go up into the clouds and back to heaven with Him. It simply says that we will go up and meet Him and that we will ever be with Him. It does not say where the Lord is going to be — and it really doesn't make any difference. The important thing is that wherever He is, we are going to be with Him.

Now the clouds in this passage are not cirrocumulus clouds — the kind of clouds we see in the sky just about every day. Meteorologists tell us about all the different kinds of clouds in our atmosphere. However, the Bible is not talking about clouds like that, it is talking about the Glory Cloud. It is talking about the Cloud of the Shekinah Glory of God. It is talking about the same Cloud that filled the temple when Solomon dedicated it, and the priests could not stand to minister but fell to the ground because of the Cloud which filled the sanctuary. It is the same Cloud which the children of Israel called a "pillar of fire" by night and a "pillar of cloud" by day which led them through the wilderness.

This is the same Cloud which came down on the Mount of Olives and took Jesus away as He stepped onto it. No one, including Jesus, could step on a physical cloud, he would go right through it. I have flown through clouds. I know that no one can stand on one. But one can stand on the Cloud of the Glory of God. It has Substance; it is the very power of the Living God

That is why Jesus could stand on that Cloud. When He left the Mount of Olives, Jesus had a physical body, like the ones we're going to have. We are not going to be caught up into the cirrocumulus clouds — the rain clouds. We are going to be caught up into the Glory Cloud — the Shekinah Cloud of God — that's what is going to cause the dead to be able to rise. The Cloud of God is so strong, so powerful, it overshadows gravity.

Wherefore comfort (or exhort) **one another with these words.**
1 Thessalonians 4:18

While the Lord wants us to comfort one another with the fact that we will forever be with Him, His Word also cautions us:

But of the times and the seasons, brethren, ye have no need that I write unto you.

> For yourselves know perfectly that the day of the Lord so cometh as a thief in the night.
>
> 1 Thessalonians 5:1,2

The point being emphasized here is that the thief does not send the homeowner a telegram announcing the time of his arrival. If he did, the homeowner would be there to stop him from breaking and entering. In the same way, Jesus is not going to announce to His enemy, Satan, the time and hour of His arrival on planet earth. He tells us, His followers, to stay ready, to watch, because no one knows the day or the hour when He will appear.

There have been people, down through the ages, who have said they have received a revelation or have figured out the date and time when Jesus will return. Yet Jesus said that no one knows that, except the Father, and that there is no way He is going to tell us. All He is going to do is let us know the signs of the times, because man is by nature a procrastinator. If people knew the exact day and time, a great many of them would wait until the last minute to get saved. Then, of course, they wouldn't be getting saved because they truly loved the Lord or because they appreciated the fact that He so loved the world that He gave His only begotten Son to save mankind from destruction. No, they would be doing it to escape destruction.

The Bible says that Jesus will come as a thief in the night. (2 Pet. 3:10.) That means that we have to stay ready by living a holy, separated life unto the Lord if we want to be among those who will meet Him in the air!

Are you staying ready?

Write: Crenshaw Christian Center
P.O. Box 90000 • Los Angeles • CA 90009.

Additional copies of this book are available from your local bookstore, or from: